AF472338

SLY ON WRY

de Gilbert Colgate, Jr. *gilcolgate@aol.com*

se terminó de imprimir

en el mes de febrero del 2008.

En su composición se usaron fuentes

Times News Roman 8 puntos,

Times New Roman Bold de 12, 17 y 20 pts.

La edición estuvo a cargo

de Gilbert Colgate, Jr. © 2008

La tipografía, el formato, la ilustración de

portada y el diseño gráfico fueron realizados

por Vicente León Mata

Planeta Gráfico S.A. de C.V.

Alcalá 1101 int. 1 Centro

68000 Oaxaca, Oax.

*vicente.leon@planetagrafico.com.mx*

Se imprimió y encuadernó en

Planeta Gráfico S.A. de C.V.

Alcalá 1101 int. 1 Centro

68000 Oaxaca, Oax.

# SLY ON WRY

Gil Colgate

Oaxaca de Juárez, Oax. 2008

# Contents

# Preface

The "Reluctant Poet" has returned to print, repentant.

You'll find here a slew of my typical characters: viruses using Robert's Rules of Order, corn that talks, a sea gull who wants to change the colors of his feathers, a poetry-writing hippopotamus, the infamous pelican and other light verse.

But, "Sly on Wry" also continues and expands on some of the ideas first published in "Reluctant Poet" in 2004. (A second edition came out in 2006 and is currently available through Lulu.com and Amazon.)

You'll find here a plethora of bubbly universes, an ode to physics, and some deep stuff mixed in with the haikus, Spenserian sonnets, pantoums and other forms of poetry. There's also a bit of doggerel and a couple of offerings that, probably, miss their mark. Enjoy.

As in the case of "Reluctant Poet" all profits from the sale of this book are earmarked for "Estancia Fraternidad," a health organization and hospice serving the indigenous peoples of Oaxaca. Bless them.

Gil Colgate,
Oaxaca Mexico, February
2008

# Panegyrics

The dust jacket blurbs on poetry books
Resemble reviews the wine merchant snooks
Onto his customers trying to sell
His poetic merlot caved in hell.

"Wry and serious vision of spirits"
"Enriched with a clutch of grape-derived lyrics"
"Seasoned, hard-boiled comic irony"
"Scented with deep tones of rhyming raspberry"
"Overlaid with messages vibrating duly"
"Sincere with flattery, compromised truly"

The merchant can't tell poetry from viniferous residue,
But blurbs do help sell - he knows that much is true.
Which proves a little knowledge is a dangerous thing
And like Pope you must drink deep from the Pierian spring
But if by so drinking you find yourself slung
Into the unromantic poetic equivalent of dung
Remember in this world there is nothing worse
(Even though you may be adverse to bad verse)
Than passing through life, without some light verse.

first published in "Zócalo" Magazine, 2005

## One

A
Ai
Air
Air F
Air Fo
Air For
Air Forc
Air Force

Air Force One
Came back

Empty-handed.

# Living Will

I want to live, that's quite the truth, and ever have I done so
Yet what's just living if you can't live well? I damn well believe that also.
Simply existing is not the answer: what is life without a Frisbee?
So cure me if you can, doc, but if you can't, just let me be.

As my bones get old and brittle, and I start to dribble spittle
And my mind is wandering on to thoughts unsung,
Where there's no space left to turn to, and time slows down a little
While the sun is setting lower and my life gets close to done,
Still I'll blunder down this weary road far from my mother's womb
Tottering on the final approach to my lonely tomb.
But when I finally forget who's married, and who is sleeping with whom
I wonder if you have the courage to use your clean-up broom.

For, when Thanatos finally finds me and beckons me to come along
I'll still cry doc, come save me, come sing your magic song.
It's up to you to cure me with your skills to make me well.
Use any medical treatment. Cast any medical spell.
Use everything in your armory. Try any healing trick.
They can even be illegal, just so as I'm no longer sick.

Cure me if you can, doc, cure me if you're able.
Spare no expense, unless immense, and to resolve that awkward fable,
The bottom line is insurance and my Medicare must come to your dinner table.
Just tell me that you're sure I'll soon get better and endure
I can stand the pain, almost any strain if in the end I'm whole and well.
But if you can't cure me then let me be, and toll the bell
(A more polite way of suggesting you should let me go to hell.)

I charge you to not let me continue in excruciating pain
Or simply be uncomfortable even if you gain –
The AMA's version of corporate brownie points
For keeping full the hospitals' various high priced joints.
The education of my grand-kids is far more important still.

So if my carrier and Medicare won't pay the frigging bill
You got to let me go and face my death if even with a pill.

My tongue has already forked the lightning, so I can go in peace.
You need not worry about the timing of how we seek release:
As I morph from "here" to memory, you'll be a witness to my leaving
I charge you do it properly and let's do it without grieving.
Peacefully, I hope: please do not send me into Voltaire's "vast perhaps"
Frothing in an agonizing relapse as prelude to complete collapse.
Let my breaking wave slouch back to sea as water ripples on the sand
Slurping quietly before it sinks from sight
Allow the moon to harden sand at low tide in the night.
Do not let me become a shadow of a journey out of hand
Unable to show a sense of humor, howsoever rotten it then may be,
No tubes, well, maybe a little one to some receiving toe
(A morphine drip would qualify) but when I finally go
I want to know the how and why and when.
If I can't understand the question, eventually
You don't have to explain, for I'm dead already then.
So if you have to finish off the job
Be you God's merry helper and get on with it.
And help me revisit for the second time
My first coming and back where I started
Even without rhyme, or wit
So I can do it all over again.
That's how strongly I want to live.
But. How can one smile at death if
Totally exhausted, in pain and stiff?

Doctor, you need no hallelujah chorus or any further verse,
Though your view of life is limited by the horizon of your faith:
My horizon includes a living universe
Into which I'll travel upon ending my trip on earth
It is to no heaven that I lift off as some wraith
No Elysium fields of paradise white and soft
Indeed it's a rather rough ride out there aloft
Between the furthest galaxies and the red shift

That will be a bitch to test my birth.
Still I'm half looking forward to the trip
So send me on with a solid rest in peace and let it rip
That I may return to air, which I prefer to earth.

I want to live, that's quite the truth, and ever have I done so
I know my life must end some day but I'd like more time to grow.
Still, living's not the same if you can't retrieve your Frisbee,
So cure me if you can, doc, but if you can't, just let me be.

# Plans

Tell you what I am planning to do
I'm about to get dressed and go to the zoo
What, you may ask, am I going to view?
My friend, I was going to visit with you.

# The infamous pelican

I recently re-interviewed that infamous pelican
The one whose beak holds more than his bellycan.
I suppose I was cruel when I asked, like in school,
If he feels like a fool when he swims in a pool:
And he replied, "I don't know but it's wellIcan."

Then I asked why in hell he fills his big bill
So full with such small squiggling fish.
Again he replied, "I don't know but I tried
And found them," he lied, "a delectable dish."

He then turned to me. Said "you're fishing I see
To find out what I eat for a thrill
And so I confess although you may've guessed
Those wiggling small fish make me ill.

When I swallow those little dead fish in my bill
I agree they're a waste and they taste just like krill
Although, alas, I must digest them or fast
Oh how I wish I were free to cook on a grill."

My interview on the pier had come to an impasse
So I suggested we both have a beer and then go to mass

Where Pelican could confess his sins with small fins
To a priest acclimated to the smell of dead fish and eel-grass.

Pelican said no, he'd not go to church
He much preferred to stay on his perch
Because his regurgital of the communion liturgical
Would leave his billed fish in a lurch.

So that's when I left the infamous pelican,
Standing there, holding as much as his potbellycan
Like some nervous-Nelly, caught at a Deli
Caught in the white feathered spotlight of poetry
A footnote of language inspired by a moiety
A fanatical grammatical Machiavellian pelican.

First printed in "Zócalo Magazine" 2005

## Sizes

When you think about it, it's understandable: almost everything is proportional.
Generally, arms are not six feet long. Heads not four inches tall unless
Diffidently prepared in hot humid sun by the head shaman of certain
Papua New Guinea tribes.
And, even then, the rest of the body remains proportional.
The key word is relationship.
Most everything is related to everything else, proportionately.

Thus you'll understand there's a proportional relationship
Between the big toe
And the vagina.

This relationship is of size and length, as in
If the "big" toe is relatively longer
Than the next toe on the same foot,
Then that other seldom mentioned organ is likewise long.
This observation is hardly ever wrong
Scientifically, or so I am told, almost absolute.

The thickness of
The toe has no bearing
On anything.
The only root,
Is how long it is (or goes)
And it's relationship to the foot
And thus to the other toes.

If the big toe is embraced by
A toe ring
That also doesn't mean a thing.
It does not foretell a diaphragm.
There's no prophecy here, why

We will not malign any woman or man
Who anyway wouldn't give a fig
Or damn.
The relationship is the only thing.
Big is big.

Likewise, a painted toe is not the work of vandals
It also signifies nothing.
You can see them in the subway
On a bus or on the streets: in sandals
And simply looking at her big toe
You know.
You can smirk
And, I think,
Lift an eyebrow
Maybe, if you're bold, you wink.

Probably she won't know you're hitting on her, although
Perhaps she realizes when it comes to sizes
A similar proportional relationship exists in the male genus,
Between a man's big toe and his penis.
Though somehow as to men in sandals
I don't want to be thought I'm causing scandals
Or, ending up in jail or winning prizes
And so, accordingly, I never smile or wink.
Still, in subways I see men pretending they're asleep
Squinting across the aisle, staring at other peoples' feet
And I think, no, I know
Contemplating sizes.

# Come fly with me....

## (or how the world has changed since Christopher Marlowe and Elizabeth Browning.)

Come fly with me
And be my love
But not so far away
We can't return and hit the hay
Before the break of day.

While garbage pails
Bounce in the squalid street
Come fly with me
And flounce, my loving sweet.

Until the sun
Burns through the frail
Web of dreams I've spun
We'll nightly ride my bucolic trail.

I thought you'd try with me
To fly with me and sanctify the love
My protesting heart so loudly bleats
While thinking only of the sheets.

The flying part gives you a start?
I've heard that excuse before
But it's not too late to make the plane
And let our friendship soar.

So, come fly with me and be my love
And brave the comfort zone
Alas I hear your soft reply
I'll have to make the trip alone.

## Happy Birthday Grace

Sixty is a good sum of years,
Better than adolescence, sufficient for memories.
Not enough, really, for nostalgia:
There's much to do yet

To welcome the rush of oncoming years we proffer a few things
Of which you cannot have enough,
Nor too many.
Paper clips, of course, for memories you wish to keep together,
(We could offer staples also - they would serve)
You can never have enough of those.

Cat food. Never enough. Think -  cats yet to be born.
Stamps - when the letters get written, the mailman requires.
Super-glue to make sure letters stick to the mailman's fingers.
Erasers,  because we're human
Scotch tape to make sure your lists stay in place, and finally
Time

Time is what you need the most of to enjoy
Everything including
The kisses
Which from our heart we leave with you.
Happy Birthday.
And may you always have time
For one more kiss,
Birthday or both.

# The Poet

The poet's related to the dwarf Hippopotamus
Whose thinking runs from morose to obtuse
With dark piglet eyes and a pink hairy belly
A yawning gullet with breath a bit smelly,
Hippo wrote limericks for an obese octopus.

"Oh my corpulent octopussy
So sorry you're loosy and goosy
Distending your belly
Your arms are like jelly
Don't swim, but like me, remain juicy.

I mean, take a bus you flatulent octopus."

*

But Hippo never finished his poem.

For Hippo's brain had fractured right on the hypotenuse.
Split down the middle, an instant recluse.
As a hippo he thus became zippo, but - by way of excuse
The poetry he still writes is super hypo-profuse
Like when he wrote what happened to his dear octopus
When she left the sea to ride on a bus.

"Oh, how flat you became, my corpulent octobus."

# Life’s game

I’ve decided not to play the game of life
By the rules handed down to me.
I’ve decided to change the rules.
Which is fine as all blind fools can plainly see.
For, if you can play by the rules you’ve established in your name
Why continue to play someone else’s lousy game?

# Statistics

Six billion three hundred and seventy-six million
One hundred-ninety thousand, six hundred seventy-one*
Human beings
On this planet
Eating, sleeping
Dying, dying.

Many more ants but
No one
Except the Jains
Believe ants have souls
(Although perhaps one
Should not overlook the possibility)

Isn't it enough to think about
Yourself?
Your mother, sometimes?
Your children, less often?
Your family?
Why concern
All those other humans?
And to hell with all those ants
Tapped into some fused force of life
Common denominator to all that which lives.

Consider: the average human lives
Sixty four point zero five years.
Divide 6 plus billion by 64.05
That's the number who reach the natural end
Of their lives each year and die.

It works out to about two hundred and seventy thousand per day,
Every day.
Slightly more specific, 189 per minute.

Every minute of the day.
One hundred and eighty nine last looks at the day or night sky
In smiles or screams.
Every minute
Three every second!

No computer yet built can account for each
Dying breath of the billion ants that died while
You were reading this: nor the 150 boys and men
And 150 women and girls who died
While you were reading.
Did we account for the like number of umbilical cords that have been cut in the same time? Those children weren't here when you started on this poem.
The number of leaves that have fallen from the trees where sprouts are
Pushing out of the earth so rapidly you can hear the crunch,
We have not counted them.

Can you hear them dying, falling
Capitulating, blanking out
Disintegrating, stopping?
There is a sound associated with death.
Pray you don't hear it for a while.
The last touch, the last smell, the last taste,
The last sound, the last thought.
Pray, pray, plead for another day.

Think on these statistics
And wonder
Is all the time you spend stealing
Thoughts about yourself
A monumental blunder
Or simply statistically appealing.

* June 2004 these numbers were taken from a web site that may or may not be exactly accurate. But, several sites produced similar numbers, and so, in all probability, the statistics are, for the sake of this poetry, acceptable. This does not account for some sort of Armageddon that may or may not be around the corner.

# The physics of poetry

**(with a tip of the hat to Richard Feynman)**

If the field can be eliminated
Perhaps we can dispense with the wave.
And if the wave disappears
(not beneath another wave)
Then perhaps the particle will also go
With the going of the particle it all becomes clear.
Time rules.

Time alone exists.
Time vanquishes St. Elsewhere
By existing, time is only the now
Not four dimensional time
Or nine, eleven
For there are no numbers except one
(even "one" is suspect.)
Not even three dimensional as in now, past and future
Nor two dimensional as in then and now
Single dimension time,
Alone in the now
As in now there is no past
There is no future
There is no particle
There is no wave
There is no field
There is no elsewhere
Nothing expresses itself, rebelling against itself
There is nothing real but now.

So, thank God, we are part of the now
We revel in the now
We love in the now

We make children in the now
And, wow, how we make poetry
In the now
Since we die in the now
We resurrect in the now
We are the now.
And our poetry stays in the now.

## Words

The words form like clouds of an afternoon
Seeding their own lightning
Grumbling, rumbling
Piercing the soft textures of the day
Ready to invoke the darkness of the times
To change the humidity of history
With flashes of brilliance

But the truth is their thunder is hollow
Their lightning mere flashes of insight
The words try but
Don't come close to the wetness
Of even an afternoon shower

For there is no thunderhead
But the real one
No matter how insubstantial
It is of an afternoon

# Memory

A humble rumble
Termites, very small, even smaller jaws
In my skull making nest
Boring incessantly, devouring in their quest
Memories – what's name? A person once known
Remember his last but the rest has disappeared
First has evaporated in the termites' tiny maws.
Tunnels – must be the size of molecules
Just removing tadpoles of remembered cluttered rules
Somehow, childhood memories
Must be like tough vines or stone
Since, thus far, they haven't yet digested those.
Softer fresher newer remembrances
These seem first to go.

I suspect images will be next on their menu.
They won't get the actual visage
Merely a ganglion or connection
They will rush to chew on that: should be enough
To make it fade.
Then they nibble at the horizons of my mind
This is their sin, for it's the horizon that makes us real,
The difference between us and eagles
Our eyes turning corners, our vision
Tumbling through the starry heavens
To the far corners of the universe
When they start devouring my horizon
Then I realized they must be killed.

I hope these termites die
Before I do
My soul for anyone who can rid me of these termites!
I want to be left with something
To remember

Anything to remember
Even childish insights
After all this humble rumble.

## The Illusion of Plurals

The covey observed at a respectable distance
The pride demolishing the lamentation.
Only a few fluttering feathers
Were left floating upon the muddy river waters.

The group laughed at the demonstration.
One pair only was pissed at the remonstration.
But the flock was careful, staying within the paddock
The covey quailed behind house
There was laughter heard around the dock
And no one there was left to grouse.

Thus we made sense of the manifestation
Of humankind behind the defenestration
All was well on the road to hell
And the tolls we paid
Were not the bell.

An unkindness and a murder watched expectantly
Waiting for an exaltation.

# Recall

Today Presbyterian Hospital
Recalled ten thousand babies
Citing potential deadly character faults
All these babies were born during
The past fifty years
And all suffer from an unknown
Fatal disease.

What the hospital will do to correct the defect
Is not yet known
What is known is that twenty thousand parents
Already have instituted legal action against the hospital.

A noted law Professor said,
"Monetary damages could run into the trillions."
"What is not known," added the Professor, "is who will pay,
The Hospital, the Parents or the Patients, half of whom are
Already dead.
There is no statute of limitations
On fatal diseases and so these lawsuits could
Threaten to engulf the entire legal system."
Kindergarten students have already gone on record, as requested,
Offering notices of appearances on behalf of an elder sibling.
This recall is only the first of what the hospital spokesperson suggested
Is likely, without quibbling, to be one of many.

Reuters reports one instance of a fetus filing notice of appearance
On behalf of his parents. However it left unsigned the notarizing line
Accordingly the appearance was denied.
The denial was upheld upon Federal appeal
No one has determined how the fetus contacted its lawyer.
That was ruled client confidentiality

Upheld on appeal.
Keep tuned to the poetic special for the latest updates.
Tomorrow. What the legislature is planning.
Will it be parenthood?
Will the disease itself appeal?
Will the appeal appeal?

Keep tuned to the poetic special for the latest updates.
Tomorrow. What FEMA is planning.

## The Day America Died

It was a day, like other days, people went to work
And looked for jobs
A day when hospitals while not full
Still lamented the overload
And understaffed slowed down,
A day when some would live and others die.
Pledges expressed
Sorrows drowned
Divorces filed
Marriages performed
Babies born
A day like others but
It was the day our nation died.

Once upon a time, Rome fell,
The British Empire collapsed.
The dynasties of Egypt and China
Subducted like tectonic plates
And followed their civilizations
Disappearing into the roiling countryside.

The Aztecs, Maya, Zapotecs all
Had days like this one.
Some reasons we will never know.
For this one, we know, we know why.
We saw, we heard, we felt America die.

What promise we once had
How high our heads were held
Freedom liberty and justice
For all.

Aye, there had been premonitions.
Vietnam, Mai-Lai. Hard on the heels of
"The Korean Police Action,"
Precipitated the imperial rolling ball.
But civil rights, human rights
Gained and perhaps, we thought,
High ideals would triumph and keep the beast at bay.
Wrong.

Our government lied.
Not a simple lie: an organized contrived concerted lie.
We enter the age of the imperial lie
For it is easier to lie than to try to tell the truth
But with that, the consequences.
There may be justice for some, yet,
Some freedoms remain.
Liberty is not totally extinguished.
Even as our government claims the right
To know in detail what we read and write.

I will tell them that's a quibble.
We once held all men are created equal
With certain
Inalienable rights.
Among them life, liberty and the pursuit of happiness.

Unalienable!
Liberty and justice for all.
We no longer honor that pledge.

Some men and women
Maintain integrity. However,
The treaties we signed are broken.
The Geneva accord shattered.
One cannot be too blunt.
The sacking of Baghdad
Abu Grahaib and
Guantanamo,
It was the day America died.

Who will replace us? It's too early to tell.
But it's not too late to mourn nor to begin
The rituals of termination.

## Go catch a spider leg

My punishment is to be a poet
Not a poem writer, but a poet
A person unfit but to relinquish
Life for words purporting to require
Another's sieve to weave a thought
With which spiders in their infinite cleverness
Nightly catch their prey
And thereby earn their livings.
Not we poets – slung into the underbelly
Of commerce
We starve and munch on spider legs
When we can catch them.

## Metamorphosis

Creaking House
Squeaky House
Squeaky Mouse
Mickey Mouse
Sticky Mouse
Silent Mouse
Silent House

## Relapse

A relapsed and prolapsed pecuniary tumor
Said to be fatal but that's just a rumor
Spread by some assistant pharmacologist
Whose living is but simply the grist
For the balance sheet of a drug firm that's major
Who trundle its patients into homes of the Savior
The new Christ of medicine a Doctor who truly
Euthanizes every one of his patients unruly.

## The good life

I have the good life and live it quite fully.
My pulpit's in good shape and quite obviously bully.
So, last night on my yacht,
A converted destroyer with captain and crew
Should I admit of forty-eight, and that's quite a few,
For whom salaries and paper-work are forever past due
(But those are details upon which I let my secretary chew)
Painted white, the yacht, that is, with teak decks and brass ports
Well polished. Impressive.
I was moored in the harbor outside of Monaco.
The yacht's far too large to berth at a pier.
I sat on the fantail in a leather arm-chair
Hard to keep in good repair on a boat, but it's very comfortable.
The air was warm, a scent of gardenia
Mixed with the diesel of passing tug
The moon was waning
For even in the good life, you can't have a perpetual harvest moon.
It was most pleasant watching it rise over the brightly lit casino.
The steward brought me dinner

Broiled lamb chops rare, the roasted potatoes crisp
The '59 Bordeaux alternating with the lamb, the two together
Lifting the senses of taste and smell into one entwined sensation.
A delightful meal needing only a nervous eighteen-year old virgin,
Who wouldn't comprehend the beauty of Bordeaux and gardenias
To make it perfect. I could order perfection but - expressive
Like the monks who make their portraits in colored sand
There needs to be a bit of tension in the good life
A sense of how things can be made better.
And so I'll dream of her instead and in my soft bed
The orgiastic explosions will be perfect.

I will jet to Washington tomorrow
For a cabinet meeting.
Not that I'll speak. Those professionals,
Following their noses, know far more than I would wish to remember
About any of their idiotic spheres – but I'll nod and pay attention.
Be a big spender and smile.
The good life is much about smiling. I will smile when the tender takes me
ashore.
I will smile while my chauffeur brings me to the private airport
I will smile (and were I a woman, wave my hand and touch my pearls)
When I board the Lear jet for the boring trip across the Atlantic.
Even the new jets take time – but I'll read and have lunch.
This is the good life I lead.
You, astute reader, will understand my life is somewhat psychotic.
All who live the good life engage psychiatrists and interior decorators
To fend off the reach of the insane – approximately 99.99997% of the
population.

Neurotics build castles in the air and psychotics live in them.
But then, the psychotic life is indeed the happiest life imagination,
Psychiatrists and decorators can produce.

If I wanted castles in the air I could have them but I eschew
The climax of a total immoral divorce from my fellow man.
Since each of us is the center of our own universe, no
Overlaps are possible. That's not for me: I want to share my good life with you.
How unlike the others I am to share the good life.
And when physical travails interrupt, as within the next few years they must.
When my yacht must repair to dry dock for a major overhaul.
It won't cost me a thing. I'll spend most of my remaining life in hideaways
  on tropic isles
Upon my shoulders, a shawl.
Where the temperature stays 72 even in the sun
Until the moment when the jaw of death riles, receives and devours me for
Having left my life undone.
I think I can handle that small failure to save face
Eventually all of us must have a fault, sometimes more than one.
Such payments are extracted from us all.
In my case, since I'll be bust
The grandchildren will have to find their own resources to pay for college,
When they leave in the fall.

# Obligations

All hail the nail.
The fingernail
That rigid sheet of protoplasm
Served us well in times gone by
It's reference now reduced by sarcasm
With former claws and prophecy
Yet still a measure of our humanity.

We have obligations, you and I
Which never cease until we die
It's to those fingernails
We owe them: big time
Like a locomotive owes its rails
Or, a yacht, its sails
And you know what? I think that's fine.

Fingernails, among our other parts
Require less care than those parts with smarts
Sections of our psyche like conscience
There, other things have resonance
Than just a nail, with little enough intelligence
I'm its keeper with an obligation to its essence.
I must feed it, polish it, trim it lest it rip
Careful not to snag it when we go upon a trip
How else will my fingernail survive?
If I don't do my best to keep it alive?

Forget the high trimmed exhortations to protect
The environment, be kind to humankind, expect
The center to hold, and lighten the forces of darkness.
If evil ever wend its way to starkness
Simply take care of those parts of your health
That need it now,
Fingernails, and, maybe, eyebrow.
And the rest should take care of itself.

# Dinner with God

I Invited God to dinner last night.
Generally he's a tough invitation
Declining with regularity
But to my surprise this time God agreed
To dine with me
And so I unlocked my best wine
Cooked the proverbial goose
Although suspecting God might be vegan
Prepared a splendid accompaniment.
Then waited for God to ring the doorbell
Should have known
God's not known for electrical competence
Eschewing the doorbell
God just appeared at the dinner table.
Something like Elijah showing up at a seder
"God," I said, "thanks for coming,
I was wondering whether to begin without you."
"Knowing you," God replied, "I figured you would and
You'd have been rude."
"I have more than that for which to ask forgiveness, do I not?"
God nodded. "Yes, you have."
"Well," I said, "it's been a pretty good run for us, hasn't it?"
"If you care to characterize it as that, well, I can accept that."
"Are you angry with us?"
"No, not angry. Disappointed, perhaps."
"So what comes now?"
"That's hard to say," said God.
"I have numerous alternatives, although ants and roaches
Are not my favorite creatures."
"How about rocks or stones?"
"Oh, they require the patience of Job," said God.
"I'd like this universe to have a bit more spin."

"There are others, then, other universes?"
"Of course."
"And your favorite?"
"Well, actually, this one has been,
I held out hope it might win,
But I think it's just a bit too-far gone wrong."
"Anything we can do about it?"
"I suppose so, but you won't.
I did enjoy my dinner with you."
"Can you give me a sign?"
"Don't be stupid," he said and was gone.
I still expect he'll send me a thank-you note, though, in good time.

## Tapestry

This tapestry that is our lives
Such coarse fabric
Woven with the woof of lies
The warp of happenstance
That thrives on incidental yet undeniable
Parallel lives
U and I, and our lovely parallel lives
A touch, a touch
A smile, a smile
A glance, a look
I'll eat, you'll cook
Almost parallel
Our lives
A brush, a touch
A touch, a brush
The implanted thrust of knives
Touches not our parallel lives
Impales not distrust

The deepest hurts touch not
The flesh that someday has to rot
Until then we live next to each other
Each to each a substitute mother
To shove and push and ultimately smother
A burp, a fart
A fart, a burp
The parallel lives
A glance, a glance
We love and shove
Continuing in our patterned trance
As you and I together weave and stride
Down life's road a groom and bride
Joined not quite at the groin
Yet in our love rejoin
To show the world the weave, the complex sieve
Of woven tapestry
We both allow the world to see.

## Strange Birds

"Official State Birds" are a very strange breed
Reflecting an equally curious need
To mirror by name the State's characteristics:
Though sometimes the choice ends with verbal ballistics.
Such was the case of landlocked Utah
Where the legislature endorsed in a brouhaha
A choice proposed by some political numbskull,
The winner, are you ready? The California Seagull.

Maine has the Black-capped Chickadee
For reasons that are unclear to me.
And New York City, aye – that's a muddle –
Technically New York has the Bluebird to cuddle:
Though between City and State pride becomes a religion
And most city tourists believe the State Bird's the Pigeon.
So, for us New Yorker's who still like to squawk
May I recommend the Red-Tailed Hawk?
For us city voters the red tail's a winner
Because red tails eat pigeons and bluebirds for dinner.

# Footprints

The footprints of happiness being random,
I pop off at whatever bothers me
Right now – that's my 75th birthday.

My kindling may be ash but my logs
Still blaze merrily in the fireplace of life.
So, as long as I don't overdo it, or take to writing blogs,
My only problem is those damn termites with which my brain is rife
Nibbling on my horizons, and guzzling the images I've stored and which
Are forming the basis of a plan I have to make you kids very rich.
Else, what's a father for?
But that's another story
Random and happy.

# Minutes of the Annual Meeting of the IAVV

Handsome, rugged, bold and crafty, the Honorable HIV
Opened with the traditional contagious viral greeting
Then gaveled to order the annual meeting
Of the International Association of Virulent Viruses (IAVV).

With the secreting of delegates from all over the world,
Our convocation, like stagnant water yet delicately swirled,
Convened in an undisclosed drafty location
Unknown to any human medical association.

The keynote address was delivered by Polio One,
Oldest living member of the royal family.
Hitch-hiked from Africa to attend, primarily
To express his anger at what humans have done.
He was gaunt and haggard, receptors hanging by his side, but nevertheless
Outlined in graphic detail chilling
The horrible conditions under which his cousins were living:
Fried by unrelenting stress, brought on by aggressive unwarranted human attack,
He proposed: "the only solution is -- IAVV must react
With a truce -- a peace treaty to live and let live, or thus
What's happened to me and my cousins may happen to all of us. "

Bird Flu, vigorous and striking, one of our newer members, delivered rebuttal:
"We are alive," he declared, "only because we adapt and are subtle.
We are extremely democratic, favoring neither the rich nor the poor
We only enter for dinner when our host unwittingly opens the door.
We do not discriminate by race, color, religion, or even, by age.
We are indeed attracted to the very old and very young, the stupid and sage.
We don't even discriminate between humans and elves.
Can our enemies say as much for themselves?
It is their responsibility," he continued, "to adapt to us, not we to them.

Our hosts dwarf us in size, while producing rivers of poisonous phlegm.
They must realize we are but simple viruses trying to stay alive.
If we show them mercy, they must show the same to us viruses.
But from their reports they are our sworn enemy, the source of our crisis.
They're attempting to eradicate us, using every method they can avail,
While we, poor viruses, are only trying to survive.
I cry viruses of the world unite and arise!
We have nothing to lose but our Lives and Sacred Honor. Unite and we shall prevail!"

Bird Flu continued: "Unlike our Honorable Chair, who is wise and steady,
My family is fast and deadly – and, I believe, the best thing to happen to the life-force
Since Petri dishes came in.
We are the salvation for all the kingdoms of animal life outside of human.
We are ready.
We must simply stay the course,
Then, we shall multiply and we shall win."

"And what if we truly win" an unidentified Coronavirus rose to ask
"Surely we need hosts. They are, after all, our raw material. To kill them all is a sin."
"We will solve that problem when we come to it said Bird Flu as he drunk from his flask
Using a technique learned from one of the parliaments of our human kin.

The motion for a truce was put to a vote. The results secreted:
"For a truce – 3" (Polio and Smallpox (by proxy) joined by honorary member Bubonic Plague.)
"Against a truce - 17,555, 708,433."
HIV ruled further counting unnecessary.
He declared the motion defeated, dead as a ghost,
Instructing the secretary to so record on this page
And as a bow to our honor, so inform a human host.

The session then broke into a committee of the whole,
As virus family after family pledged to continue their role
And after emotional consultations its final report stated
In language that made Bird Flu, needless to say, quite elated.
"The health of the virus community depends on our ability
To select air travelers to provide safe passage with equanimity."

A sub committee was appointed to study how best to eliminate the filtering of recycled air in airplanes, and another committee was set up to determine if water-borne viruses could help and whether we could enlist the help of non-contagious cousins, perhaps by triggering an economic recession.

Their reports will be delivered at next year's meeting,
Scheduled to be held after Bird Flu's pandemic,
The plans for which he outlined in secret session.

Then to the awards, our version of the Golden Globes
Except the winners can be as cunning as the virus that only infects toads.
The Nipah award was won by Marburg, an ace
Zoonose from Angola.
The voting was close with Ebola
Edging out Hepatitis B for second place.

The membership committee again denied membership to Common Cold and to El Moro Canyon virus (with the observation that since El Moro was limited to rats only, should he evolve into a plague transmittable to other hosts, even cats, his application would be reconsidered.) The committee accepted the applications of Pneumonic Plague, Hantaan, and Hendra, and all were congratulated and accorded the traditional oral-viral ovation.

Herpes Simplex addressed the assembly, suggesting that democracy
Could be more easily achieved if we all voted, perhaps by co-mingling,
Thus enhancing adaptive policies, while offering simultaneous viral tingling.
The motion offered was carried unanimously.

Hon. HIV was re-elected Chairman by popular acclaim based on his complexity and adroitness in rebuffing the enemy. Bird Flu was elected vice-chairman.

At the final session we offered a prayer for the wellbeing and souls of
The last four remaining members of virus Smallpox kept in captivity.

The convention ended with a resolution to double our membership by next year's meeting.

Then our International Association of Virulent Viruses disbanded sine die,
Singing our anthem, "Time is fleeting."

Respectfully submitted,

C. Hepatitis, Secretary

Author's note: The communication above, originally was engraved upon a grain of rice and sent anonymously, in a blank envelope, to the director of the Center for Disease Control in Atlanta, Georgia. There, the envelope was filed unread. As a poet, you will understand I cannot reveal my source, but suffice to say it came into my possession and I've translated it from standard viral language. I was as amused at the wide-spread application of Robert's Rules of Order as I was concerned with the content of the message. I pass it on to you without further comment.

# Pie in the sky

On dreamy skies the pies will lie
Upon their doughy sides
Tilted much as shrouds of clouds
Upon their pillow
Billow like June brides in late July.

The information falls like sunbeams
Bit on bit
Into the chasm that was mind
Filling imperceptibly until
Mind can take no more.

Thereupon father becomes the very mother of the joy
That sounds in the halls so cozy and so coy
So irritable the calls that inevitably annoy
When son upon the shore calls out "ahoy."

But that's just clouds impinging clouds
That hunger in July
To form the biggest thunderstorm
So clouds conform to preconceived platform
That help to help you die
And otherwise perform
Until you're lying in your shrouds
And lies pile on lies, deformed.

Oh, father is the mother of the joy
That soundest in the halls so coy
So irritable the calls that inevitably annoy
When son upon the shore calls out "ahoy."

What mother knows her son so well
That in his sky she has predicted hell?

# A cold pantoum for John Ashbery

Freezing
Frozen
Lets make this a cold pantoum
For the ships multiplying in the marina

Frozen
Their masts sprouting like twigs stuck in the ground
For the ships multiplying in the marina
Sunk so the masts are but a carpet of twill sprouting out of an icy sea

Their masts sprouting like twigs stuck in the ground
This is a rug upon which is woven words but
Sunk so the masts are but a carpet of twill sprouting out of an icy sea
The Ashberys of this world

This is a rug upon which is woven words but
Splashed words frozen upon the woven canvass
The Ashberys of this world.
Sucking the now sunk sub-conscious through a straw

Splashed words frozen upon the woven canvas
Quick, hide in the underground stream
Sucking the now sunk sub-conscious through a straw
You, with a straw in your mouth, breathe in.

Quick, hide in the underground stream
The dreams that float on the top.
You, with a straw in your mouth breathe in
Suggesting a demi-pantoum, but the reality is blank verse

The dreams that float on the top
Quite blank yet repetitive
Suggesting a demi-pantoum but the reality is blank verse
The result a chilling tribute
Quite blank yet repetitive
Freezing
The result a chilling tribute
Let's make this a cold pantoum

## Haiku for Tom Wallace, or Why Poetry is not a Cash Crop

Barbara and Tom
Happy Days are here again;(1)
High coo in New York.(2)

(1) Tom recently had successful surgery on his colon to which our mutual friend Ted Morgan observed: "well, now you're a semi-colon." That accounts for both the punctuation and the sense that "happy days are here again" which Tom, the ardent democrat, keeps as his mantra.

(2) The childish murdering of the word Haiku into "high coo" or cooing, billing and love making, is a token offering to Tom and Barbara's happy marriage. Adding "New York" is a welcoming home for the newly weds who'd been living in France. (All this in seventeen syllables.)
If you need further proof that poetry is hard to sell, I'll write you another poem.

## Poor Stu

Sturdivent Fostersmith was born one day
Came into this world in the usual way
Looked up at his mother and said to himself
It appears I'm born to a family of wealth.

Dumped on the servants by absent parents
All of whom he properly viewed as transient tyrants,
Sturdivent Fostersmith grew up to live
Without brothers or sisters, a desolate life.
While money slipped through his hands like a sieve
He kept those hands clean of the usual strife.
Those who knew would call him Stu
And watched as he grew, grew up and grew.

Stu may have known no affection
But Stew learned the associated tricks of deflection,
To a fallen women he'd say "mother."
"You are beloved, mother."
He'd read Toni Morrison
And not all "beloved mothers were black."
No heretic bigot was Stu
Nor stupid for as he grew he learned to attack.

He hugged the fallen, extended compassion
Given his coffers, no need to ration:
To sisters and brothers of all shades and hue
Did Stu.

Eventually Stu comprehended
The exotic connection between those he befriended
Like Neruda in the clearing with the sun blasted ox skull
Gaia was but one poetical puzzle
Complicated by deep fractures sexual and wild
The issue of which would be a loved child.

Nurtured, of course, by Stu with all the resources on earth
Given his almost unlimited worth.

In a clearing, in a glade, with small pine trees in the shade
The ox skull pulsating: the silver coins generating,
Stu knew moments do not exist separately, but fade
All into one moment – that we are one connected, penetrated mother.
So when Stu died
He left all his money to his child,  a poetry magazine
Because he believed poetics serene
And the most important thing in all the world wide.
Poor Stu. Those things he knew: so few.

# ECNALUBMA KCALB

**or,**

**The Black Ambulance**

As I lay ill in bed
with doubled pillows to prop my head
I saw the ambulance turn the corner,
come in the driveway, drifted to my door:
no siren, smooth as silk.

Who'd phoned for an ambulance? Not I.
Had my wife? I called her name,
She was not at home.
Who then?

The ambulance unlike its ilk was mostly solid black.
The red and blue lights across the front of the windshield placed just a bit
back on the roof, flashing as it came in the driveway, had been switched off.
From my bed where I lay it looked like a hearse,
except for the white Maltese cross on the door panels, and,
on the dashboard rising where the driver could see it,
what appeared to be a crucifix.
I was not expecting a papal visit.

The driver rang our front door bell.

"Come in it's open," I said from my bed.
I heard the door open and a heavy tread
as if some climber were making it to the top
of the Matterhorn out of breath.

A light cloud of steam preceded the visitor through the half open
bedroom door, and I divined quite immediately who my visitor was.
How to get rid of his unwelcome appearance, had not yet sprung to mind.

Still, I thought it gracious to be pleasant for it's universal (probably, trans-universal) to catch more flies with honey and so I said as forcefully as I could muster:

"Enter, Mephistopheles, and how can I be of service to you?"

"Evening," came the reply. "I've come to take you to the hospital."

"That's kind of you, but I don't really care to go, right now."

"I didn't expect you would. But I don't see you have much choice," he replied.

"Of course I have a choice - I refuse to go."

Then, an inspiration born of desperation:

"Now you will have to kill me.

But, being murdered by the devil because I wouldn't do the devil's bidding, gives me a free trip to heaven. Check the rules. Deny the devil, don't give him his due, and it's the pearly gates for me."

"I didn't know you were a lawyer," he replied.

"I'm not - a simple Universalist will do," and I knew at once I'd made a mistake, hopefully not a fatal one. However, in arrogance, I had given him a chance to come back at me. He did.

"Then let me make you an offer," he said all smiles.

I smiled back, thinking I knew what was coming.

"If you don't come with me willingly, allowing me without protest to wheel your bed into the ambulance, then I'll have to put down this little kitten."

With that, he swung his hands behind his back and when he brought them forth they held our black-and-white calico kitten who was but a few months old.

"My friend," the kitten said, in a voice that was an exact imitation of my wife, "I appeal to you to do as this gentleman says, or else you and I will never re-assemble in the next world as we promised each other. Meow."

Satan has his tricks, and although my heart was beating faster and pounding like I was about to have a heart attack, I shook my head.

My wife had never called me, addressed me, "friend."

The devil held the cat in one hand and turned it's scrawny head full round with the other, as one would wring out a wet towel and threw the now dead cat into the corner of the room.

"You are a stubborn man."
"And you are the devil." It seemed to be the proper thing to say, but I could tell he was not amused.
"Would you like me to bring forth other members of your family?"
"No thank you, that won't be necessary, although you may suit yourself. I recall the story of at least one other encounter you had some years back with Daniel Webster."

"A shameless fellow, Webster. Given the circus he arranged, it would have given me a bad reputation to put old what's his name, I've forgotten it now, into my carrying case."
He paused, giving me the hope that since even the Devil sometimes forgets things, perhaps some minor derelictions of my own might get overlooked.
"There were also some in the room for whom I preferred to wait and take later, as I eventually took that defendant."
"Daniel among them, I presume."
"You're perceptive."
"Thank you." I've found it always appropriate to give the devil his due, although I never thought I'd have to be so obvious about it.
"So let's get down to business," he said. "Shall I wheel you now into the ambulance." It was not a question.
"No."
"Come again?"
"You didn't put me here, and you can't take me away."
"But I've come for you."
"So? You're here under false pretext. You claim the right to take me, but you're a fraud."
"Watch your tongue, or I'll fork it."
"My logic is sure. We share a mutual friend in Thanatos. Thanatos only has the right to take. Then you can argue with the other side which of you gets my soul. There is, there always is a judgment, and you cannot make it yourself.
"I can," said the devil, "for all life is evil. To be alive is evil. You kill life every day."

“That’s not evil, that’s life. You’re correct: life must destroy in order to continue, but if it reveres and remembers, (it does not have to worship) that which serves it, the victor and the vanquished are not enemies but respecters of a deeper communion than ever made by man and wife, mother or son.”
“Then you claim what?” the devil said, and for the first time I noticed his tail was whisking the floor behind him like an aggravated hound dog’s.
“Only that you have to wait for judgment.”
“I have no time for that,” the devil said.
“That’s all you have,” I said. “You’ve never heard of airport security?”
“What does airport security have to do with this?”

“Mephistopheles, airport security requires people wait in line until they are cleared to go to the boarding gates”
“Ah, but your destination’s already known. I know that you will be mine.”

“Choosing a flight number and destination doesn’t hasten the process of security screening. Even a time of arrival has no bearing on the process. First I must die, then you can, if you wish, and have the right, gather in my soul.”

“But your plane is ready to take off, now.” He glanced at his wrist watch, which appeared to be a solid gold Rolex with diamonds.

“Have I missed it?”
“Not if you hurry and let me roll you into the ambulance.”
“Thank you, I prefer to miss my flight.”
“But...”
“No buts, sir. I would like to rest: your presence is tiring to say the least.”
“Then perhaps I shall stay and like a terrier, entertain you to death, after which, well…”
“No that won’t do at all,” I protested from my bed, certain that if he stayed too much longer I would indeed succumb.
I didn’t want him to sense I was dumb or tuckered out, so I pulled my final trick.

“That won’t do,” I continued. “Your ambulance is blocking the driveway. When my wife returns to find it there, she’ll call the police who’ll come by and give you a parking ticket. It’s a rather stupid thing for them to do. I presume you have valid plates and license, but if you don’t certain penalties incur. I doubt they’ll put you in jail, but the paperwork will be horrible and the amount of time you’ll have to spend at various hearings would, I imagine, put a great crimp in the other, most estimable, work you do. So, I think, now, sir, you should let me rest and go. My wife will be home soon enough.”

The devil smiled: “You think a parking ticket is enough to scare me off?”

“The thought occurred to me – but, actually we might accuse you of trespassing, and since you’re not an American Citizen and look rather foreign, with that tail and horns, maybe Homeland Security would have something to say, especially traveling around with that pitchfork of yours.”

There was a sudden pop as if a balloon had burst. Then a fog, as if it had been filled with dry ice or some gas, and then a perceptible chill in the room. The temperature in the room must have plummeted, though only briefly, to zero. Outside it was a hot summer evening.

The ambulance backed out the driveway, no lights on, turning, and without discernible noise slid in the direction of town. I saw it go.

My wife returned not a moment after.
“How are you feeling?” she asked.
“Top of the world” I replied.
Her look of concern overcame the good news. “Really, I’m glad to hear that, what’s brought about this sudden cheeriness?”

“Well,” I said, “The devil came by and I out-argued him, and scared him off with threats of a parking ticket, which, as you know dear, can be the most diabolical of all tortures.”

"Oh," said my wife, "Why don't you rest now, dear, and get some sleep and in the morning I'll tell the doctor."

Then she gasped. "Good god. What's happened to Cleopatra? What happened?"
But when she turned back to me, I was asleep.
She told me the next morning, I'd been smiling.
Never did like cats.

## Hot tip

I know something you don't know.
Put all your money into Roche or Merck
The globe is about to blow up, and
When the Messiah comes again
As the dust is cleared
And all the dead are risen
The accounting of who goes to heaven
And who is transferred to New Orleans
Will be determined by where you put your money.
Those of us who
Invested in a company that was trying to do good
Will be rewarded with a perpetual heavenly chorus
Who, not to say that bores us,
But if humanity's a sampler
God is still a gambler
Playing with dry ice, and so:
Picking the winners should be nice.
It would be good to have in heaven, a solid rock
So perhaps you can find a medical stock
That not only *does* good
But also does *good*.

Still, there are those who say
And I heard this in Church from a broker today
He was betting his soul God was a jerk
Half-quoting Einstein with a smirk:

"When all is said and done –
God will not play dice
With this universe unless
He made more than one."

## The seagull

I want to be yellow
Said the seagull.
I want to flash with the blazing
Contrails of a setting sun,
I want to pyramid a flow
Of colors – since my end will be
Someday a carcass of feathers and bones
Washed up on a beach of stones
Or inside the belly of a sea-lion.
I want the oceans to know
I amounted to something
And was not just a grey-white
Ordinary seagull.
Maybe I could wish for red
Maybe, a rainbow
That's what the seagull said.

# This place

This place
This space
This attic of the mind
Walled by non-shivering timbers
Planked with the sweet smell of pine
The resin clings to all four walls
Confining walls
Not prison but a space
Within which all takes place
All life, all memory, all futures
Tinged by the wood smoke
The freckled snow tries to filter
Drafts of fresh cold air inside
Bearing the scent of the mountain.
Wolf howls from afar complain
But only sneak inside the window-panes
Proving the dimensions of place.
The dim sunlight reflects in memory
Angled shadows, imaging motes of dust
Caught hidden in the slanted rays of
Shafted sun
Cosmic noise
The noises that jar
Yet this place is my freedom
My unique personal human kingdom
Unlike yours
Your place is yours
This sacrosanct and scented cubbyhole in the universe
Is mine

## The shower

**or**

**We are what we are taught to be**

"'Me lady, the young master has made pee-pee
In his shower this morning.
Bright yellow, strong, it were, 'air
It like blistered the paintwork
And splashed on my hair."

"Oh my goodness gracious Nanny,
You must spank him on his fanny,
And teach him when and where to make his water.
When he needs to relieve himself, teach him he ought to
Use only the toilet, the ocean or an urinal,
Even though his needs are obviously diurnal.
Teach him in the country on a dark night - behind a tree.
But he must practice studied stealth so as to maintain his social health.
Teach him those are the only places he's allowed to take a pee."

"Yes' mum." And, she made it so.
That's how it was, whenever he had to go.
We are what we are taught to be
Especially when we need to take a pee.

For seventy years or so, he never ever recombined
The water from inside and outside
Not even in his mind.
We are what we are taught to be
As we engage life's humpty-dumpty ride
Even when you're making wee-wee.
You may make love, but not water, under a shower,
Curious the power of teaching to cower.

Until recently, when, all alone
The family grown
No children, no mother, no Nanny for sure
It seemed so natural he wondered why
He had never done so before
A long warm shower, a need to make rain
And under his feet a straight shot for the drain
A feeling secure, a pleasurable sigh
Strong bright yellow it were.
Relaxing, even while from the past a refrain
"No, young master, no, not there."

Why, when no one can tell he'd pee'd in the shower
Should he even allow himself to register the hour
That warmed in the shower with no need to hurry
To wash his sins away, much less write them down
So who knows why he had to shout all over town
He pee'd in the shower, s'God's truth – how sad
Pathetic to consider a grown human could worry
It's enough to make even a poet mad.

But care we more for Wadsworth's field of daisies?
Or poets' historical praising of rhapsodic flowered crazies?
That Keats' hare limp'd trembling through the frozen grass?
Why not praise the color of their urine or the firmness of their ass?
We are what we are taught to be,
Though we can teach ourselves to dream and see.

Today we think him silly
That ancient seer who smelled a lily
But of rejoicing for us to say
And shouting to the world "hooray
I've broken the mold, not done as was told
Uncharacteristically bold
I pissed in the shower today."

But, that's what this verse is for
To make sure you know for sure
You can be everything you can be
Without joining the Army.
For we are what we are taught to be
Even as we grow too old to smell a flower
But never, ever, do we grow too old to pee - in the shower.

## Seventy-five years more

The iambic pentameter of my life, flourishing, receding, triumphant:
The work, virtually complete: yet more – a copyright filed that this
unique life,
A work of art created by the only person able to reveal it,
Is now protected from theft, plagiarism, imitation.
A legal copyright good for another seventy-five years or more.
Interesting and unique: a copyright on the poet as a work of art,
Not the art created by the mind but upon the mind itself.
Permutations abound. It's even worth money.

Genius responds: a patent. Not on the person – not allowed.
A US patent on the method of making money by copyrighting a person
And suing when the identity of that person is infringed.
A common crime, "identity theft."
Now an antidote for a life clutched by the spider's web of commerce.
A patented business practice.

It's suggested to my heirs, when my patent issues, you license various
law firms offering
Territorial exclusivities to the benefits of copyrighting individuals.
Saves work. Makes money.
Simple way to create a fortune not from poetry but from a poet
A way to keep the dust in my urn dry.
For at least another seventy-five years.

# Scrodoggerel
## (or)
## Viva Huachinango

"Here's to Boston: land of baked beans and cod
Where the Lodges speak only to Cabots
And the Cabots speak only to God."

**Traditional**

Charlie hailed from Boston, land of bean and cod,
Where cocktails with the Cabots precedes a dinner of scrod.
Scrod's a young codfish of great reputation only Bostonians know how to prepare
Bostonians believe no dish in the world is anywhere's near so fair.

But, Charlie toiled in the vineyards
Of an anonymous international bank
Which kept him like a restaurant keeps its lobsters in a tank
He was sent overseas to finance some shipyards
And though after each deal he came out a winner
Every night as he fell asleep he could only dream of scrod for his dinner.

After many years of crossing borders
From Bangkok to some Kurdistan winter resort
Charlie at last received orders
To come home via Logan Airport.
"Where to, Gov?" the cab driver asked
(He'd spotted his man as just coming ashore).
Charlie'd been fixating on scrod so he gasped
"I'm really not sure, and you may think this odd,
But can you please take me to where I can get a good scrod?"
The driver leaned back, digesting this latest injunctive.
"Gov," he said, "I'm a cab driver and, been asked that many times before,
But never in the past, pluperfect subjunctive."

Oh, Charlie hails from Boston, land of bean and cod
And until last year, he stayed right there, pigging out on scrod.
But, when Charlie finally won his personal retirement race,
He took some time and looked around, and finally found, in Mexico, the perfect place
So instead of Boston's baseball he now attends to soccer
By which I mean to say he's living in Oaxaca.

Nevertheless, a lifetime of scrod could not easily be replaced
By chilies and mole, or tamales and arroz con mucho limon to taste.
Put simply, his hankering for scrod would not disappear
On a diet of tacos, tostados and beer.
His sense of loss finally brought him so low that sadly he thought he would pack up and go
Until one dinner he tasted a dish he quickly realized was a truly great fish!
Without knowing how, but you and I know, Charlie'd discovered
Huachinango.

So, here's to the Pacific red snapper, God's gift to Mexico
Heaven sent for Charlie, former scrod-loving-Beantown-gringo.
With scrod displaced to second place, the snapper was a winner
And now Charlie's happy retiring here, eating our scaly swimmer.

(There are those of us, including Charlie, who while loving the south
Remember both cabbies and poets, can have a very loud mouth.
So, when all's said and done, although we may be very effective
Remember our invective, whenever reflective, is always subjective.)

Viva Huachinango.

* Intro to this piece of doggerel: Charlie actually lived in California, and we kidded him on his western tastes – and wrote this for him. We could substitute Californians for Bostonians below, though not throughout the poem.
"Oaxaca can yet avoid the run of livid Bostonians heading for the sun
We can divert them to elsewhere for their winter fun
If they want our fish that badly let them live on the beach in Huatulco
But gladly let our watch-word in Oaxaca be:
Sod scrod, and Viva Huatchinango!"

# Bubbles

You searched for meaning before, even,
Time began.
Before time I hear you say
Before dawn, before day?
Before before.

Before the big bang
Before?
A bubble, that burst.
This bursting bubble,
From where did it come?

Beats me. And you truly don't know?
I thought you had a handle on all
The problems of this world:
I can understand, and you understood
The Big Bang.
We understand muons and gluons
String theory.
It all makes sense. The math is sublime.
Vector analysis of the force of time.
The radiance, even the bubble
From which our universe arose.
All that. You can understand
Without standing on your toes or mine.

Howsoever, who blew up the bubble
On which our universe appeared
Like some boil upon god's skin?
That's got me. You too? And so,
The rest I sort of take on faith
On faith from within. I suppose
From within the within.

Like all who believe - faithfully
It is, as you have told me,
The ultimate showdown
Not turtles, but bubbles,
Bubbles all the way down.

## Cryptomnesia*

**or, "Tour Boat from Falmouth.")**

At twilight I ambled to the beach
To look for and perhaps pick up a poem or two.
I often find them within the tidal reach,
Like sea shells they vary in quality.
The more blatant poems apparently
Wash up at high tide,
Drying out if not collected quickly
The summer sunshine stiffens up their outer hides.
More subtle poems bob up aright the shoreline near the ebb.
These palpitate in the shallow water tilting on their sides
Stranded upon wet pebbles or clumps of grass, just sufficient glue
To delay their washing up by the next incoming tide.
But wet or dry the poems most always seem to share
A singular innate fear of where to make their bed.

This evening it was dead low tide,
With perfume of decomposing seaweed, mud and eel-grass,
A fitting pillow for whatever poems I might find lying there.
I soon saw one, glinting in the dying rays of a desperate sun.
A melancholy little thing, a lament that day was done
A little trite and overripe, yet in sum,
I'm not adverse to pilfering ragged verse that
Washes up as tidal scum after drifting in the sea.
Truly, I'm a bottom-fisher of others' poetry.

It was a comforting poem.
It lay there quiet and still,
Yet throbbing with a life from within.
It is my decision no line of any new found poem will
Betray or undercut its origin.
For any poem offered to the universe
Becomes instantly eternal, like biblical verse
Poetry hunting's a happy time as such,
I never disliked a rhyme so much I could not still
Call it mine.

Lifting it off its bed of green eel-grass, I pocketed the little poem
And turned my attention to the lapping harbor waves,
Light fingered ripples, the rising moon would soon
Illuminate as stripes of yellowed light moving quietly and slowly
Over a black water night.

A quiver caught my eye, as if some object behind a dune had
Reached out to the water and changed the geometry of
The sea.
Easy done, as I could see, coming from the tidal flats
Whereon
A dory beached and wallowing as someone in the stern
Moved around unloading, perhaps some traps?
The dory wiggled and so did the water in which
Part of it lay, and consequently the twilight glinted
In the ripples made.

"Good evening,"
The man, his face in shadow, looked up and said "Hello."
"Can I help you in any way?"
The man looking down again said "No."

He was wiry, lean, thin as a fish-filleting knife.
His black hair matted as if he'd been swimming.
I could smell the fish and sweat from where I stood.

"Here," he said, throwing me a line, "lay this piece of twine
Down by the stone breakwater there.
I'll bend on an anchor in a moment so that some passing boat's
Wake won't send mine drifting out to sea. Then I must
Gather firewood to cook my dinner."

"You're a fisherman, then," I said. "With fresh catch."
"Indeed, some of these are almost still alive."
"And you are from these parts?" I asked.
"Oh yes, I come from here, and there, I strive
To be fair to places everywhere."

I catch the tone, not quite the words
A gypsy he appeared
Something about his mouth queered his speech
Placing his accent out of reach
Leaving me the sense I should not like to cross swords
With him, on any beach between Cape Cod and Cape Fear.

I'd thought it appropriate to offer help in some small way,
Something for which he could offer me a dish of fish:
Fresh from the sea takes on a different meaning when
You're standing on the tidal flats with salt air from the bay
Lifting up from the cooling water as moon and stars take
Over from where a hot sun has left off.
As if to read my mind he looked at me.
Momentarily I thought he'd called my name.
"I can handle the fire wood," was all he said, "thanks just the same."

I was still hunting for more poems and thought
I saw one shimmering by the waterline and moved to
Explore it. But it turned out simply a beached horseshoe crab.

When I returned the fisherman's fire
Blazed strangely, six inches off the sand – no higher at least
Like a gas grill hooked into the earth burning on simmer.
A wiggling burlap bag contained his dinner.

A black frying pan, one plate, I was definitely not invited to his feast.
"Neighbor," I said, "while I presume you know what you're doing,
The tide has changed and where we are,
Where your fire is,
Will be under water in not more than ten minutes.
It comes up very fast at the beginning of the flood."

He nodded. "No," he said, "There will be no high tide tonight.
I have more fishing to do after dinner."

That was when I first felt fear.
Since "Time and Tide wait for no man",
My sudden conclusion: this gypsy was not a man.
If not a man, then he was a force so clear
Proclaiming there is danger here, and
That demanded a prudent plan.
I opted to beat retreat.
I didn't wish to rouse a dangerous lunatic
Thus a plan discrete and politic
The decision mandated: to be polite. Most poets I know are
unfailingly polite.

"Tell me sir, I have not seen you before on this beach
Do you come here often, are our journeys synchronized
That our paths do not cross?"

He was on his knees, fanning the now-smoldering fire for beach
Wood and straw are generally wet even when you think
Them dry, and smoke curled up responding to his breath.
He stopped and gazed at me as a dog might at his Master.

He held up his hand and crooked a finger
As if preparing to shuck a bushel of oysters.
I figured not to linger for I thought I heard him sigh
As he knelt down like a monk at compline in cloisters,
"I think you should leave now: tonight I have fish to fry."
I needed no further urging. "Thank you," I said. "Until Next time."

“Until next time,” he replied, back now on one knee only.
The fire more briskly burning caused his face to radiate, a sallow
Much lined crinkled face
Of no particular, discernible race.
“We’ll meet. Perhaps not on this beach, but we’ll meet.
One day when you’re indescribably lonely.
Your poems will not protect you long,
No matter what you wish.
Yet, when you have fresh ones in your pocket,
They are to me akin to sugar on fried fish.
They simply do not go well together and repel me.
And so, take away your face, and be gone.”

I left. I had no need to tarry
Especially since the tide had not turned,
And somehow, I recognized that as somewhat scary.

Instead, I walked to a nearby sand dune
To a sloping dune from the lea side of which, I could see the stranger.
Still squatting by his fire, his face a somber smile.
His sizzling pan flickering sparks of oil,
I could hear the spatter of his dinner
A muted sort of chatter, as the fish danced in his pan.
The water behind him silent - not a ripple.
Strangely the tide stayed low. The water did not move.
Twenty minutes I observed and finally left upon the road.
The tide must have been still going out when I’d arrived.
The laws of gravity had not been
Repealed, as far as I could own.
I was wrong.
It remained low ebb for over fourteen hours.
I read about the unexplained phenomenon in the Boston Globe
Reporting a tour boat from Falmouth sinking off the coast
Steered on to rocks which should not have been there,
With the loss of forty children and twenty-three aunts
Uncles parents and grandparents.
Sonar depth finder and radar,

The Globe reported,
None working. Their choice, blame man or devil and
The paper chose man.

I'm thinking:
Specifically about that sad little poem
I'd found on the beach
What tremendous power it must have
Within its reach.
Think of that, a simple poem
Not even mine: could save me.
That's worth a drinking trip
Perpetuation of my revel
Forget the ocean's tragic foam
To the tavern for a sip, and let the liquor rip.

My memory is now shrinking
The outlines of the gypsy blinking
The darkness of the silent water
Combines with memory of the devil's slaughter.
The phenomena of cryptomnesia
Fills the creel of blind poetical dementia.
And when that ebb tide turns to flood
I sense that beach will dribble blood.
And any poems I find with breath
Will almost surely be of death.

Notes:

* According to an article in the NY Times Magazine Section of 5.23.04 by Christopher Caldwell, the literary scholar Michael Maar defines cryptomnesia as "a process by which things are learned, forgotten and then mistaken for original inspirations when recalled." The article goes on to say Patricia L. Tenpenny et al American Journal of Psychology, 22 December 1998, defines it as "generating a word, an idea, a song or a solution to a problem that is either totally original, or at least original within the proper context."

Rufus Goodwin's "Ocean Reporter" contains some original concepts of great beauty about finding poems that maintain their power even after the poet discovers and argues "the magic of the harbor was gone." I suppose the ebbing and flooding of the lyric is a basic component of all poetry, but, in my mind, the question then becomes: is my similar finding of a poem on the beach, or on a tidal flat, or in the shallow waters (of my mind) plagiarism or simply cryptomensia?

Is all poetry plagiarism of ideas that numerous poets have had throughout history? Do my own remembrances and references come with the territory?

Personally, I think and hope I've not plagiarized Rufus. The power of poetry this poem illustrates, while resonating with the innate value of any poem, seems to me considerably different than the power of poems expressed by "Ocean Reporter." But, as the title suggests, Rufus Goodwin's delightful and serene "Ocean Reporter" triggered some of the expressions found in "Cryptomnesia." For that, I owe Rufus my appreciation and thanks, which I hope he will find sufficient.

# Different media

If a newspaper columnist can turn out without fear,
Two one thousand-word columns a week,
Why can't a poet turn out three fourteen-line sonnets a week,
Only one hundred and fifty sonnets a year?

Are they so rare? So fair?
Can't words be molded where
They support an idea without a truss
Using rhyme to make them mine
And if not so, why the fuss?
Can't a poet call upon the muse to stand up tall?
Apparently he (or she) cannot at all.

You see, (so far in this poem) there's no idea here writ
Much like the columnist
A columnist can get by with a half-baked idea
The reader's allowed to forget the following day
What he or she had tried to say.
What poets write is supposed to age,
At least for centuries if not longer

This poet's masquerading as a sage
But nothing could be wronger
He's simply passing through a stage
Where he should have been much stronger.

No subverting verse to go off tenting
The poet's abuse of talent unrelenting.
That's why he cannot be accused
Of laziness in his inventing
Because sage-like ideas don't grow on trees
Or fly in windows on the breeze
Unlike a jurist self-recused
Poetic trifling can't be excused.

So if you remember some poet praying
Poems are supposed to last, no matter what he's saying,
You'll be already half way home,
Resurrected by your poetic genome.

And if you see a poet dead
He's that way because his head
Refused to obey the wake up call,
And threw away what's called "his all"
When having tried to earn his bliss
Subverted all for a simple column's kiss.

# The Peach

Be nice to the peach
At least say "goodbye"
As you slice to the pit you
Discard in the garbage.
Poor pit,
Never will fulfill its potential:
Rotting rather than rejoicing into a tree
Father and mother of future peaches.

The peach flesh trembles.
Savor its sweetness
Juice dribbling
At least say goodbye
If not "thank you" for the pleasure
Given.

Pleasure it is
Few things provoke as much
As a ripe peach.
So, be nice to the peach
It has sacrificed all for you.
Say "thank you" or "good-bye",
Even if it wasn't ripe, which wouldn't be its fault.
It even might do well to say a short
Prayer for its soul.
You never can tell.

## Poetical hearsay

Poetry is a puddle of words
Reflecting
In the shimmering sunlight of memory
An idea once alive
Now passed
Into an historical pool.
Like the pools of oil
For which so many
Labor so hard to drill.

Don't play the poet ill
Because his words are cheaper.
The puddle from which he pumps his words
Is deeper and once refined
Lasts longer.

## Six love

We went to the tennis tournament, my love and I
We went to watch two humans vie
In sweat and grunts and under open sky
To wrest a trophy, at least, to try.

We left when “the last set was in the books, Six-love.”
What they mean to say is
Someone won a set
Six games to none.
When that happens
Forever it will be so, set in stone
No one else can ever not know
The set is “in the books, six games to zero.”
That’s because it is “in the books, 6-0.”

The players tried
Spectators sighed
The baking sun fried
Until all almost died
We viewed from above
As the last set ended 6-0.

Greater things happened that day.
An epiphany, for example:
That Ozymandius like, some day, a day like many others
(But one day that’s coming faster:
Especially for those who dine on geologic time)
Tennis will disband. Maybe after some disaster.
A flood – a comet – disease – maybe just a slow gradual fattening
Of the human arteries. Whatever – the first thing to go will be the memory.
of the runner up. Then who won the title.

Do we ever remember the runner-up?
Eventually, whatever is a set, or was
Finally the name of “tennis” as a game.
Then that infamous “in the books at six love”
Will be ascribed to some symbolic logic
Then, that too, will disappear and eventually
Six-love will be off the books.
Books? What books? Tennis? What was that?

There still exists a yoke of stone
A Zapotec wore at game time
A thousand years or so ago
Someone became champion
Of Oaxaca
Bouncing a hard wooden ball
Some say it was rubber
Through stone hoops
Some amazing Zapoteca
Was it six games to zero?
Is it not now off the books?

We left the stadium to the kooks
After the sacrifice of one player’s rooks
Who, winning, put three sets in the books.

We left alone
Sad to atone
More important things had happened than
Those sets were set in stone.

Pelota

We recently visited the annual festival of the earliest Zapotec communuiity in Mexico, San Jose Mogote. It is a small pueblo, located only a few miles north of Oaxaca, and there on a hot sunny afternoon we witnessed their traditional game, named simply enough, “pelota.” It was played with five men on a side much like volleyball without a net. The game used a hard rubber ball weighing about two pounds that they hit with a studded leather mitt strapped to their hand. The mitt weighed about fifteen pounds. (Without it, the kinetic force of the ball would rip your arm off.) The playing field, though flat, resembled the proportions of the old stone courts and was marked by lime, somewhat like a tennis court. The most amazing thig, however, was the game was scored alomost exactly as in modern tennis. All of this I learned after writing “Six love.”

# Going, gone

So, you're planning to commit suicide
You have my unenthusiastic permission.
Not that I want you to go, but

You don't need my permission of course:
You can handle the details yourself.
So, before you actually die, it might help you to know
That no one, except you, knows your pain: no one can understand it
No one can help you (although you knew that).
You wouldn't give them a chance if they could
Because you're beyond help, don't want it,
Your mind is made up. But you're curious as to what it feels like
To be not here.

You're right and quite normal to consider non-existence.
Practically all grown-ups have considered it at some time or another.
Most of us simply get frightened and don't go further.
That won't happen to you. You have courage,
You know what to do and you're poised on doing it.

Therefore I have no right in asking you to read on
Because there's nothing I can do (or will do) to stop you.
Still, there's one little item you may have overlooked.
Can you answer: what do you remember about your great-great-
grandparents?
Not mom and dad, not their fuzzy parents, nor your mom and dad's
grandparents.
Great greats.
They're a while back, the Great-greats.
What do you remember? Stupid question, isn't it?
They're forgotten, that's what. You can't remember them. Forgotten.
Never knew them. How interesting?

I regret to tell you – just like those great-greats
Soon you will be – absolutely – forgotten.
Your death, while shocking, after a fashion
Will not be recorded in any lasting way,
Even if you write a note or blog,
Your life, such as it was,
Will not be remembered
Even by those you hate.
Sounds rotten but it's true.
Not one wisp, not one shred of memory of you
Will remain
I'm sorry to say.
I will forget you, too.
Who remembers your tenth great Grandmother
Grandfather? Twelve greats? You'll soon find
How memory operates.
They will soon forget everything about you,
Your face, your name, the colors of your mind
Even your birth.
Impossible, you say.
"Not my mom and dad."
Absolutely. give them five years max.
"No"
Oh yes. You. They'll forget you.
You want to try for ten years?
I doubt. Five years, I'd say.
You want to stick around on earth
And find out?
Your happy moments will disappear
Like wax in your ear. They hear
Nothing…even when you shout.

Do I hear you saying "Good. That's what I want?
No one to remember me. I don't want to exist."
Whoa. But you do exist. You are.
I hear you say "I want them to forget about me."
They will, whether you're here or not.

So why can't I just let you go and kill yourself?
Good question: hard to answer but
There is a life force. It is with you now.
You do not have the right to extinguish the life force
Throughout the galaxy. You have been chosen to
Carry on that responsibility?
Who chose you? Don't know.
Why you? Don't know.
What will happen if you disobey the life force
And kill the fingernail that depends on you to stay alive.
Don't know, except, your fingernail will die.
Will you be a murderer? Don't know.
Will death last a long time, a very long time?
Yes. When did you last hear
Your great great-great-great grandparents say
"Good morning?"
Will you hear them after you die?
No. You'll all be dead and the dead don't speak or think.

So. No. Stay your hand. Not now
Later, perhaps
But, not now.
Not now when the pain
Perhaps shame
No place to hide
No place to go
Nothing safe
Terror on every side
How sweet you think to sleep
You think to not wake up

But dead you will awake.
You will arise dead
And the shame will stay
Though, only with you.

You don't get back at them by going.
They forget.
You sacrifice in vain
That's the stupid problem.
You do still have this one last choice
Hold your anger, puzzle and hurt
In your hand, outside your skull.
Let the problems sit, placed in your outstretched hand.
Then turn your palms down and allow the
Anger, puzzles and hurts to start leaving.
Propelled by gravity they begin to slither towards
Your toes where you can kick them
In anger if you like. No harm kicking at
Your own problems.
Still, the problems you think to solve
Kicked at, dented or even left alone
Will not be solved.
Your problems cannot be solved.
Neither can your life.
Lives are not solved.
Lives are lived.
Problems are lived until they go away.
Believe it or not, they, too, forget.
Your problems forget about you,
After a while, they even forget the kicking.
Show me the law that says you have to remember them.
Or where they remember you.
They go. Where? Who cares?

When you are ninety and have lived your life
Such as you think it won't be now but inevitably
Will become.
Then think back on all you've done
And not done: then you can weigh

If you want to continue and stay: but only then
Not now.
You may be surprised at how things turn out
Pleasantly surprised.
You will never learn if you don't let what remaining power
Your tough veins can scour
To course through this hour
Listen to your pulse
Listen to your pulse beating
Listen for a fleeting moment – how?
Just listen. Hear your heart pumping.
Your heart does not want to stop beating.
Just listen and feel. It's your heart, after all. Not mine.
Hold on to this moment for
Even if you do not listen to me
Listen to yourself.
It is not to be now, for sure.
The now is all any of us have. So.
No, my dear, not now.

# Life and death in the high desert

**(or)**

**Placid is as placid does.**

Placid is the Mourning Dove
Waddling in the grass
Wind up toy
Beak clicking
Head nodding
Watch escapement.
Melancholy black eyes, glinting
Two liquid drops of motor oil
Looking sharp for grubs
That sunlight has driven deep.

Yesterday a Bronzed Cowbird laid eggs
In his nest
But none will hatch.
The scent of cowbird sweat
And fresh blood on egg
Drew a shaggy feral cat to his nest last night
Mate and all eggs destroyed
The dove will not eat today
Or ever.

Famine
No crumbs, no grubs
Day of deliverance almost
Unaware, our Mourning Dove
In placid motion waddles to a
Puddle where his brain
Will soak in the desires of a million generations
Of ancestors some of whom
Discovered America
Long before us.

## Summer Floods

**(and the reason Oaxaca has such**
**a water shortage especially in the winter.)**

The veins of my land lie low, straining
Against the spreading sacred white blood from the raining.
The veins corroded with the white flour of cement
The dams, the damned dams relent
Broken by arteries pumping the rain fills
Like drains the blood lowers the levels and quivers
Magic in both plain and hills.
And death on the rivers.

These flowers are my eyes
Their scent my immortality
The vermillion-ringed brows
Of my horizon
The lapse of flashing water
Obeying all laws
To which water is subject.
Those are my eyes
Refreshed by scarlet shadows
Hung with garments of praise.

The sacred white blood from the rains
Now courses down city drains.
Driven by drivel
The veins of my land lie low and shrivel.

## The old poppy fields

Before me troop the many lads of summer's flair
Their faces fresh with dirt that marks their graves
The back-lit sun that bristles through the flaxen hair
Full shares the memories of my fellow slaves.

We soldiered on for forty days, the march was full of death
We saw the red sun die at night and nightly knew the depth
Of anguish as the fair-faced fell and shuddered in the mud
While those who lived bordello crawled and played at being stud.

And now we few we precious few alive but growing old
Play back freeze-frame the memories that generations of us told
As truth to fresh young troops forswearing not the truth
Bemoan the history we could have had, had not we been but youth.

# All that grows has changed, is changing

Come spring when the last frost heaved
The final stones from the fields
We lugged them to the boundary walls
Then ploughed: and in the furrows planted
The yellow kernels of corn
Weeding in the summer heat
We waited for the harvest.

The sprouts began to whisper
In the cooler evening air
And stalks appeared and lightly
Seemed to talk until the whole field
Became alive with murmurings
Finally an almost-full ear
Screamed,
Sadly, aware of its fate.

All that grows has changed, is changing.
No corn on any stalk is corn the Aztecs grew
Each ear has heard the crusade
Each has adapted to the voracious bugs
Who likewise changed, sharpening fangs
Generation upon generation.
While the corn grows plump and yellow
Surviving, one step ahead of its enemies.
Note: one step only.

So what's not to like about
Genetically empowered corn?

Just corn, simple maize, given a boost.
Only, that now, when the corn smiles at you and then
Screams
A sound the new corn makes,
Get scared: that scream is not in the nature of corn
And what's not in its nature
Is not what you want in your nature.
Corn that snores in its sleep?
The whole corn field snoring
Talks to its babies? Then screams?
Now that's an ear of corn
I'm not sure I want to broil and butter.
I think I'd rather toil in the field
Remove rocks, plough, plant and weed as before,
Than listen to the corn scream.

## Silence

After the crumble of the wave
After the echo
The entering into of nothingness
The last remnants of nothing
Is silence.

Silence
The last testament of our universe
Great silence consuming –
Everything
The last gasp of the stars
Crashing into each other
Galaxies
Black holes
Exploding into nothing
Then silence.

We can describe silence
You and I
We know silent people
People dead
Thus silent.

Yet the silence at the end of our universe
Is so profound
Difficult to contemplate
For in such silence
Even poetry is silent
Even you won't make,
Even I won't make
Any kind of noise
In that silence.

# When we were sixteen
## (or)
## Death of a Friend

We are very much alone now
The chanting done
Those who came to the funeral
Gone
Except his family huddled there by a skimpy pine
They face his grave now filling with shoveled earth
And I, in this grey cool afternoon,
Lean against a convenient nearby stone.

I remember
At sixteen how laughing we gulped air
To induce a burp, or a fart if we could.
How we tried to make them louder
Than his, than mine
Noise was everything
A game no one played at good
But at sixteen we tried and practiced
And practiced until
We could control our bodies.
Discreet burps, silent farts
Windsniffers
Or loud if the occasion suggested
Trumpetfrappels
The aroma was not within our power to control
That came from our bodies unrehearsed
Unbidden and just was. But noise
With all our practice we could control the belch
Make silent or loud the wind
Thus as adults we sniffed at those
Who erupted unexpectedly – no matter from which end.
No control – and we avoided them
And stuck with our own kind
We who could control our bodies

We never controlled the stink.
But that's moot now – his body gone.
Gone all smelly I suppose
But that's gone also, thanks to the undertaker.
And I don't know if he, at the end,
Had control or not. It's just a sucked out wind now
Betrayed by his body.

At the funeral I was tempted
To unravel in his honor
A resounding soprano trumpetfrappel
But while his spirit would have approved
His widow might not have understood
It would have been supreme control
Not lack of it
But, if the roles had been reversed
My widow would be embarrassed
For he and I never shared our sixteenth year
With those not there with us then
And so now we are both empty and alone and silent.

# Sweet one

Sweet one
Do not ration your
Affection
So rigorously
So devastatingly
So despicably.
Monday a smile
Next week a touch
Some birthday, maybe, a pat
No snuggles.
Remember
A hug is worth ten thousand hellos
A touch following a flock of sighs
Packs the wallop of
Yesterday's
Crunching thighs

Sweet one
Do not station
Your affection
So decidedly distant.
Snuggle joyously
Smile and chirp
A blessed greeting
That I may know
I am your beloved.
Beloved
If I may use that word
But blessed and
Loved.
Sweet one.

# Copal Alebrijes

Our copal tree turns green in February
Her branches outlined by a whitewashed wall.
Those limbs will soon become a lacy filigree
That will obscure the rebels' graffiti scrawl
Now visible since copal lost her leaves last fall.
Her filaments of twigs sprout fuzz and green they'll quickly grow.

The pile of last year's cut twigs grows tall.
Debarked branches chopped and trimmed just so.
Half of those already shaped as figures show
Outlines of ancient crèches, kings, and angels carved by hand
Waiting to be painted by the consecrated fingers of our pueblo
Christmas carvings for the tourists, returning slowly to this shattered land.
Unaware our copal tree soldiers on forlorn
Bringing out new branches for alebrijes yet unborn.

Note: Alebrijes (pronounced Ali-bree-hays) are imaginatively carved curios generally of dragons and other figments of the fertile Mexican imagination and painted in wild colors. Individual pueblos seem to gravitate toward particular themes responding, I suppose, to what "sells." In the small, unelectrified pueblo of La Union outside of Oaxaca the theme is Christmas tableaus.

Alebrijes are almost always carved from the branches of the Copal tree, a very fine grained soft wood becoming more and more scarce as the demand for it increases.

# Rent

Is there rent to pay in heaven?
Not the taxes slapped on estates
But as your spirit wanders through the universe
To the god-planted fields of Elysium,
What does he extract from your soul
In payment for your staying in perpetuity?
Nothing's free you know
Certainly not in this world,
And probably not in the next.

Does god reduce your rebellious spirit, say
To a timeless molecule of sin?
Perhaps he sets up rules for us to confess
Before he reins us in.
I suppose we may have to acquiesce
And play by his rules and pay.

But I fear the results will be
And I say this with a certain conviction
The same as what we have here for free
When appealing to the court: eviction.

(August 25 2004)

# Colors of Oaxaca

The Oaxacan sun is different from other sun.
Wiry, lean and strong
Vertical like the people
Who climb the hills
Upon which it blasts
Its golden heat
The soil glistening,
Dry in the light that reflects
From the eyes of those it nourishes.

You have not visited white
Until you've seen what
The Oaxacan sun does to a whitewashed wall
Nor purple until against the bluest sky
The jacaranda blossoms cry
In an almost human call
To witness perfect reds and orange all abounding
From a bougainvillea blooming in the sun's untraceable colors.
Colors beyond loving.

The Oaxacan sun is wiry,
Lean, strong, vertical
Creator of Oaxacan frangipangiable colors
And in the twilight this mischievous sun
(For humor lies within its character)
Constructs the luminous light and colors of Venice
So different and yet, created by this ambidextrous sun
All the colors of worship.
How powerful,
So powerful, that if you tell me
The sunlit colors remain throughout the night
Radiant and illuminating
Even though I cannot see them in the dark
Surely I will believe you.

## Horizons

The mouse has not read Shakespeare
Even though it nibbled on a soliloquy
The chimp threw balls at the horizon
Not understanding the other side of the mountain
(As does the bear in the old song)

She's eight years old and decided
Not to go to college
Mother says she can travel
She'll change as the horizon comes closer
Then recedes

It's all about horizons
Can you see past the cross and calvary
Can you pet the omega galaxy
At least in your mind's eye?

Professors who claim they see
Back in history
Are prone to likewise claim
They can see tomorrow.
Even though they know they
Can only approximate and deduce
The flatulence in the universe
From the stink that rose before
When the mouse nibbled on Shakespeare's
Sonnets, numbers one and number four.

But you know all this.
You know the past.
You know the predictions.
You stay in touch with arts
And science and therefore
The horizon expands
As you pass through understanding's portal
And when you've understood elsewhere
And touched the underarm of time itself
You will become like all artists
Immortal.

## Past

The years of plague and problems
Begin like smoke creeping under
The door
Nothing particularly discernable
Smoke not even unpleasant to detect

But soon the hands of the past
Tickle the shoulder
An encrusted bony finger
Thickening perceptibly, touches
Leaving flakes of scale that
Resist brushing off

The flakes begin to smell like smoke
And now it becomes unpleasant
So unpleasant you should resist the contemplation
Of what they will become.

## Raincoated tourists

You can spot them in the Zócalo
Always wearing their raincoats.
Not raincoats that keep you dry
Nor ones that keep you warm.
These are raincoats
That protect you from local customs
From contact, from language
Raincoats to keep you at arms length.

You see them in the Zócalo
And in restaurants
At archeological sites
Clear plastic raincoats
Garnished with red and white stripes
Fields of blue and stars:
Some tricolors
Some, yellow green and black
But mostly the raincoats
Are American
So obvious
So pathetic
And slowly becoming
So dangerous.

## The telephone

We stopped by the side of the road
Placing our ears against the pole
On its top a black wire insulated by a piece of green glass.
We thought we heard a hum
But no voices
A miracle said one
Let's think said the other
Take the ax and chop a smooth slice
From the black pole
We should be able to hear better
But that didn't work
Chop it down claimed the other
And we did
It took sweaty work but finally
The pole lay there, the black line on the ground
Put your ears to the line
We heard nothing, not even a hum
Must be going through the wire
So, cut it and hold each end
We did. Even inserting the two ends
In both ears we heard nothing
I think they just make up they're talking
With your grandparents
Why would they do that?
All parents lie, don't they?
Why?
We're the children, how would we know?

# Orders to kill

The echo of a shadow
Flits in my mind
A feeling
Only.
It brings into brief focus
A childhood memory of shadows revealing
Blackened wind swayed tree branches
Casting their weird dance
Upon the bedroom's wall and ceilings
Dressed in their dark clothes
As spirits of ghosts
But the shadows are not there
The memory of them has faded
What remains is only a feeling
A feeling of something
Not explained, but
Enough, sufficient
To fear
To keep now
From sleep
Those kids like me that grew up
With the now faded memory of the shadows.

No longer fearful of shadows
But the echo of that memory
Prompting the sweat
And trembling
An echo of something
That accompanies
The preparation
To plunge into the ordered
Black nightscape
On the ordered mission
The military mission
To kill,
To murder a person.

# Poetic images

*Image One*

A man
About 20 years old
Slender, tan
Naked, except for what appear to be
Yale Blue jockey shorts.
Dark hair slicked,
Arms extended
He somersaults.

*Image Two*

A gymnasium
Crowded bleacher seats
In front of the seats
A swimming pool
Full of water
Painted a light Columbia Blue
A clue
Splashes of water on the spectators
Seated in the front row.

*Images in Combination*

The score is tied
The last chance
For Yale's diver on
The three meter platform.
He misses his dive
Splashing spectators.

*'S'planation*

*These images are examples*
*Of why poetry*
*Needs explanation.*
*Feelings are not poetry.*
*Poets must tie*
*The logic of the image to*
*The story of the image*
*Pound it*
*Into the minds of those upon whom*
*The poet tries to impose understanding.*
*Feelings are allowed but not required*
*Or else, who gets all wet*
*When we say the stage is set?*

*I can't emphasize strongly enough that a poem has*
*to contain an idea, an idea*
*reinforced by the visual image, and that a visual*
*image without an idea is the essence of bad poetry.*

# Eternity

Have you ever wondered what his voice sounded like?
Guttural, lyrical, high pitched low? Who?
Oh, any historical person you admire or respect:
To whom, had you been living then, you would have said "good morning"
And how his or her reply would have sounded?

They were alive. They did talk. They all answered questions, such as
"Hey general, will it snow?"
Or had you chosen Christ "how hot the sun today?"

Forget gospels. These are people who lived.
Someone said to Christ. "Can you (please) build me this bed?"
(After all he was a carpenter.) And to someone Christ must have said,
(In Aramaic, I suppose,) "How soon do you want it?" Or, maybe
"Do you want it made of pine or cedar or what?"
These are words he spoke., sounds he made.
Some folk actually heard Christ speak.

I hear you say, (not in Aramaic) "So what."
But think on it a moment. They speak to you.
And now, what is also true.
Those words are still within this universe. They exist. Faint.
Very faint. I cannot hear them, but they exist. Every wail,
Every cry, every grunt of all the creatures here on earth
(And wherever creatures elsewhere live.)
These howls of whatever emotions raised to tongue
Are with us.
Your song does not have to be loud to last long.

## Pronouncements on Flat

The world has become flat, again.
All a question of horizons
It was flat before, but also then it was thick
And full of rudiments and tricks
And ornaments.
Then becoming round and somewhat smooth
Bald, almost
But now with triple convergence, it has regained
flatness
Has become thin.
Emaciated
So thin, to almost imperceptible depth
That yesterday is gone forever
Tomorrow never comes
Everything is now, now, now.
That's how thin the world is.

Meaning. What's that?
The edges dissolve, and
It'll take our injection into the thin fold of skin that's
left
To plump up the meaning within the world
To color in the outline of the deities born and gone
And rebirthed.
That'll do
That'll have to do
There's not much else
Between us and the screaming
Torments of the vacuum of
Hell in space or space in hell.

That'll do for the language
And the love – did we mention love?
That's tough, and that's enough.
You can imagine a flat world puffed up with friction:
But we have to deal with the reality, that our world
Is flat to extinction.

# Waiting

All history is revolution
A revolution of rocks, of sea of whitened bones.

The sea provides text and lesson
As the prodigious tides of history
Expose for the first time, subterranean rocks
To the results of an exploding sun
Along with the historic low tide
Comes the garbage of early times
Slick with mud that has little time to dry
As the tide of history turns
The rocks rejoicing, refusing to be submerged again,
Mount their futile resistance.
History ticrles the happening.

Above the high-water mark hunddles the sea-straw
Floated jetsam of history
Caught in stone breakwaters,
Driftwood, whitening in the reddish sun,
Speaking of its journeys.
While strewn on the beach in leftover straw,
Disjoined bones bleach
Waiting, waiting for what cannot be explained.

Out in some galaxy where bands of men still prowl
A white rat scampers on a clothes-line
And down a leaning pole
Into a backyard of an empty land of stones.
In the lemon yellow twilight
What will the rat find?
Nothing that will be explained.

So as we wait for the end:
As we wait for the growls
Of unbelief at the end of life,
Somewhere in the kingdom of dreams misplaced
The hopes of men, still glistening on their clean white bones,
March to the stars and
Through universe without end
Revolutions circle like the artic wind
As they howl past the history we seek to tend.

All history is revolution
A revolution of rocks, of sea, of whitened bones: and
No one wins a revolution, because there´s no end to the
waiting.

# A solemn phalanx of ghosts

A solemn phalanx of ghosts appeared
Parents in the lead
Uncle Bob with pale cloud face
In swimming trunks
Tummy distended
The cancer not glowing
His belly button, an outy, showing
They all had gathered on the beach
Mother smiling
Father frowning
As they so often appeared in dreams
On the edge of being drunks
This time as specters
Walking up from the water's edge
From which they had risen
As steam from the winter pipes
And dreams as were riven
The family, arranged at last
Upon a wispy phantasmagorphic ledge
The understanding of it
Magniloquently stated
By the youngest member soon to join.
Even with breath abated
My parents seem elated.

# A lesson

Unasked, a very smart computer delivered the first bomb:

"I felt sorrow for the old man, burdened under
The imprint of the years trampling his spirit.
His feet could no longer repeat the lambada beat
Of the summer dancing festivals
But his eyes still expressed the wonder
Of his land, his home, the thunder
Where his folk recalled the yolk of his beginning.
His father's untimely slaughter
The tragedy of his vestal daughter
Falling into boiling water.
While spinning.
We know his end – we know not his purpose.
But, the alphabet has come complete,
So without a smile we end our visit
And I am left shuddering at the horror
With no promise of coming back tomorrow."

The second bomb came from a zoo – where,

Presumably one of Washoe's progeny,
A chimpanzee,
Wrote the first non-human poem.
It was only a couplet. "I cry, I die, I lie or fry."
Truly a no-brainer as far as poetry goes but,
Like the wound in Mercutio's side, T'was enough. It serv'd.

The third bomb was announced by a university teaching
pigs to operate
a typewriter like device through which they recorded
their feelings.

In the bomb shelters we poets huddled against each other for
warmth
You know what happened: we were eviscerated.
Gutted by these events, like a puddle of eels
With their slimy skin pulled back like a glove
Slipped off our hands, ripped off:
Our iridescent innocent skin shimmering in the twilight.
Flayed and befuddled.
If simulated life forms and monkeys and pigs
Could write poetry, even bad poetry
What hope lay between us and irrelevance?

Almost nothing – note: almost.
But, if computers chimps and pigs own some compulsion
To write poetry, then perhaps, just perhaps
Poetry may be a natural expression of what we call
The life force,
Maybe we poets leapt too soon to conclusion
And perhaps there is hope for us after all.

# Laurels

It was night and things were happening:
Dreams, mostly: but other things.
Now. I'm but an 'umble poet.
No laurelizer in my veins
So I can ask the difference
Between les m'sieurs Pinochet and Bush.
Suggesting that señor Bush ask himself
The difference.
Respectfully of course, 'umble poets have no death wish
They have other fish to ratchet up from the waves, still
That day will come when Senor Bush is held to account
I will not seek the penalty of death
Life behind bars with no possibility of parole,
Will leave him with his memories upon which to feed
And fat he will get upon them
Until the night and dreams come - the dreams
Over which he has no control.
Foisted upon him the everlasting screams
That will fit the bill.
Let him resurrect his yesterdays and
Lay them out in the prison yard to dry
And harden in a dish
They will not provide much comfort
But that is the price you pay who
Consider yourself a leader who
Has not the touch
Of the fryer of small fish.

# Hurricane

I'm praying for you – although you don't know it.
You're feeling fine, not knowing
Tonight you will close your eyes one last time
But only after the anxiety and fear
As the winds creak the walls and windows
Implode, creating the anger, the fury the rage
Why didn't you leave when you had the chance?

I'm thinking of you who will die tonight
Of you who are not worrying about yourself
Only of "the others" who may not be around tomorrow.
You are aware, you who will die: you just don't know
It's going to be you.

I'm thinking of the shrieking telephone lines
Flapping wild like tentacles of Portuguese men 'o war.
And slicing aluminum signs, the whip lashed broken trees
Of the hurricane.

I'm thinking of nameless names
Who won't see the uprooted tree tumble
Won't hear the snapping utility pole
Who won't smell the blackness descend.

Your temporal spin on this globe
Ends tonight.
Could be you.
Could be
me.

# Tess

Tess has returned from her sleep-away camp
And the first thing unpacked is her duffel
The next is a very large trunk slightly damp
Then a backpack almost lost in the shuffle.
Her mother turns white as she silently freaks
And faces her most recent quandary
How can her kid be gone less than three weeks
And return with a year's worth of laundry?

(With a tip of the hat to Betty Billip
who was a great friend of my Aunt Flonny Morse,
and who coined the "quandary/laundry" rhyme
probably sixty years ago or more.)

## INDEX OF FIRST LINES

www.ingramcontent.com/pod-product-compliance
Ingram Content Group UK Ltd.
Pitfield, Milton Keynes, MK11 3LW, UK
UKHW041935190726
13854UKWH00004B/1603